# THE NUTCASE ACROSS THE STREET

Reflections On American Politics

**THE NUTCASE ACROSS THE STREET**
**Reflections On American Politics**

ISBN-13: 978-1478262978
ISBN-10: 1478262974

# THE NUTCASE
## ACROSS THE STREET

**Reflections On American Politics**

**DANIEL NOE**

# Introduction

My name is Daniel Noe and I am an American citizen. Like most of you, I am nobody special. I work full time for a living. This is my first book. I'm not a politician, nor do I plan to be, but I *am* interested in the political affairs of this country.

Like many of my fellow citizens I am concerned by the amount of political strife in our country. Public debate seems to become ever more vitriolic and the populace seems to become ever more polarized. Hateful, prejudicial, and downright nonsensical statements spoken by my coworkers, friends, and family about politics make me question their judgment and doubt that I can ever trust them – with anything. What is wrong with everybody? Or alternately, what is wrong with me? Ever since I was young I was very curious how and why people thought differently. That two people, when given the same information, would come to different conclusions was a fascinating phenomenon worth studying. When I grew up and learned about politics, I was stunned by people's behavior. I understood selfishness, but I never understood why one would go out of one's own way, even to one's own detriment, just to hurt another.

From what I have heard, these are the feelings shared by many: that most of our fellow Americans are hopelessly deranged and must be defeated at all costs. Republicans hate Democrats, Democrats hate Republicans, Libertarians hate both, and communists, environmentalists, and islamofascists want to overthrow the whole system. Politicians of all parties lie to get elected, sometimes even politicians we otherwise like and support. In the meantime, we try to do the right thing by staying informed, but it is difficult, and many of us are not sure who to believe anymore.

This book is about how systems and individuals keep us divided, why they do it, and what to do about it. I believe that most people are reachable if we could only understand each other.

I wrote this book in the hope that it will help us do this. To understand and be understood are fundamental emotional needs. I hope to meet them. I not only write this book for you, but for myself. This book is largely a story of how I attempted to reach out to those I disagreed with, and what happened as a result. Perhaps if it works for you, you can do the same.

# The Current Conflict

We live in a divided society – or so people keep saying. It is hard to listen to the news these days without somebody claiming that the United States is becoming increasingly polarized. Tales of riots and intimidation abound. ACORN protests AIG (1). Tea Party activists protest congress. Politicians continually demonize each other and their talking points are repeated by their supporters at home, school, the workplace, and the marketplace. The less stable among us fly small planes into IRS offices (2). George W. Bush has often been criticized for saying, "Either you are with us, or you are with the terrorists," when speaking of regimes that harbor terrorist groups (3), but it was former presidential candidate Al Gore who claimed the 2000 presidential election was a choice between good and evil when speaking about himself and his fellow citizen George Bush!

(4) What are we divided over, and who is behind it? Republicans blame Democrats. Democrats blame Republicans. Independents blame the media. Traditionalists blame waves of immigrants and multiculturalist attitudes. Progressives blame the establishment and prejudicial, exclusionary attitudes. Capitalists blame the centralization of power and decision-making. Socialists blame the unequal distribution of wealth. Fundamentalists blame moral decay and the erosion of the role of religion in society. Some people blame everybody.

Whatever the source, this division is generally perceived to be a growing and worrisome problem. This, in turn, drives a growing pessimism of political affairs that only acts to deepen such strife. I have wondered for some time though, is it really? There is always bound to be some minimum level of strife because of the divisive nature of some of the issues we face today. Is there more than is to be expected or just the necessary amount? How much strife is there, and has it truly increased in recent years? How does one go about measuring strife? Finally, how big of a problem is it? Does it even matter?

To begin by answering the last question first, it does matter. It weakens the bonds of society. When one cannot trust others, we all suffer. Have you ever been friends with someone for years and then discovered that they were "one of them"? Did you wonder about their judgment after that? When political strife increases, political issues and our stands on them become more important. This drives apart friends and families.

To give an example, abortion opponents argue that terminating a pregnancy by aborting a fetus is no different than infanticide. As an opponent of abortion rights, if you truly believe that, how can you trust someone to babysit your kids known to support candidates that oppose protecting the unborn? Not seeing anything wrong with abortion, might they not also see nothing wrong with infanticide?

To give another example, capitalists argue that the government has no business regulating prices. "When a seller is willing to part with his goods for a certain price, and he is able to find a buyer willing to pay that same price, it is no business of the government to interfere with our fundamental freedoms by changing the terms of the deal to favor one or the other," they say. To them, the minimum wage is akin to stealing. If as a capitalist, you truly believe that, how can you ever trust someone known to support candidates that vote for minimum wage increases? Would you lend them money? Not seeing anything wrong with price controls, might they not also see anything wrong with stealing?

Yes, you can spend time with these people. They might even be fun, but can you ever become close friends with these people? Can you trust them? Can they trust you? Will you ever receive true sympathy from them? Will they ever really understand you? Can you understand them? To understand and be understood are fundamental emotional needs, but personally I find that my concerns are largely misunderstood and ridiculed by those claiming to be my friends.

It was some time ago that I read <u>What Triggers School Shootings?</u> by Michael S. Kimmel and Matthew Mahler for a sociology class. According to the research, kids (and people in general) are more likely to react with violence when they feel that they are not even being listened to, let alone negotiated with, and when they have no other outlet. Just one true friend is usually all it takes to survive high school. Just one person who accepts you is enough to find the strength to ignore others. Reading this immediately reminded me of our current political situation. Our government and elected officials ignore us, doing what they please, and dismissing the legitimate concerns of millions as the ravings of a few fringe lunatics. They don't listen. Even among opposition groups, the members are usually only united around a very few issues. True, long-term friendships are thus impossible. Given the immense numbers of important issues, this is a continual threat to the stability of these groups.

I keep finding that I don't fit in anywhere. I am not a Democrat, a Republican, or a Libertarian.

I'm just frustrated. Judging also by the reactions I receive from others, and the way they treat each other, I'm not alone. Nobody fits in. We are all mad at each other. It is under just these conditions that violence becomes more likely.

Political strife also has the effect of curbing information flow. To make the best decisions, we need the best information. Sometimes others know something we don't and we know something they don't. This is why open discussion and information exchange about politics is so important, but when division and anger sets in, many withdraw from discussion completely and become private about their beliefs. Some become discouraged about the whole political process and drop out. This leaves the rest of us talking only with people we agree with, creating an "echo chamber" of ideas, and stunting our education. This is a very dangerous situation. It allows corrupt politicians to play off our fears and mislead us. It also increases strife, feeding back into the divisions and deepening them.

As people drop out and become ever more cynical, fewer people are left doing the work of self-government. With fewer people keeping tabs on our political elites, the more out of control they will become. Corrupt officials are more likely – I believe – to act badly when they perceive that only few care. Don't stop caring!

In extreme cases, of course, strife and alienation breeds militia groups that threaten to overthrow a divided government. We aren't there yet, but we are headed in that general direction. I may not be happy with the current political system, but I would prefer not to initiate its violent overthrow. Revolutions often end badly, causing chaos as rival groups vie for dominance, with the new regime often times being worse than the old one.

Revolutions become much more likely when the elites make up the rules as they go along, live by a different set of rules, or are believed to have the whole system rigged. In today's current political climate, even the very institutions used to mediate conflict are disputed. States' rights advocates are quick to point to the tenth amendment, which explicitly limits the federal government to only that which is explicitly stated in the constitution. Legislators pass laws deemed unconstitutional by many. The president wages wars without congressional declaration. Was the September Fourteenth resolution a declaration of war? People disagree. It is no longer even enough to leave the interpretation of the law to the Supreme Court, because the role of the court is itself disputed. "Activist" judges legislate from the bench. Even scientists can give no final verdicts that are not then challenged by scientists of differing political persuasion. Global warming, evolution, nuclear energy, and medical marijuana are only a few of the scientific controversies of the day. Finally, when election results are disputed, widespread rebellion cannot be far behind. When it is perceived that the other side is not even following the rules of deliberative engagement, some will see no other alternative but violence.

Clearly then, there is potential for great problems, but is this situation avoidable – or merely an inevitable consequence of events beyond our control? In the following chapters I hope to explain this in greater detail. For now I will simply say that you already know the answer. Rather than sticking to their own messages, politicians and activists seem to feel a need to misrepresent the messages of others, insult them, and in some cases completely destroy them. This is not necessary. It is a deliberate act that alienates whole sets of voters while misinforming followers, and therefore sets the electorate at odds with itself, unable to have a civil debate on issues alone.

As for my final question as to whether strife is on the increase, I have yet been unable to determine the answer. There seems to be no universally agreed upon way of measuring strife among sociologists. My personal impression has been that there has been an increase, but obviously I experience only a small part of the world like everyone else; it could merely be a statistical fluke. This is especially so in my case, since a large part of my experience is listening to opinion show news analysts who continually claim to see an increase in strife. When it comes down to it, we don't really know, but it seems likely.

It is in this current climate that various "tolerance movements" spawn. Politicians will decry our deepening divisions and present themselves as "moderates" that can "work with the other party" and "compromise". If you listen closely, however, they always seem to find someone to blame for causing our current divisions, and they often accuse those merely exposing the ugly truth of being among those driving the division. The issue of divisive politics has itself become a divisive issue!

Take political talk show host Glenn Beck for example. Some would characterize him as one of those driving us apart with his constant criticism of Washington politicians, but those who actually watch his show know one of his primary threads of discussion is how those Washington politicians drive us apart by bringing up minor issues so they can collude together on much bigger things while we are distracted. In other words, he criticizes others for being overly critical. Beck often encourages us to get along better and be more tolerant. He is clearly non-partisan. He doesn't support any one party. He may pick on Democrats more often, but this is likely because they are still in power, and tend to be slightly worse by his standards anyways. The point is: his standards are constant.

Jonathan Haidt (Department of Psychology, University of Virginia), is a leader of a different sort of tolerance movement. Drawing from his theory of moral foundations, developed with Jesse Graham, he states that our political attitudes derive in part from our moral values, which in turn derive from our genes. Since there are so many conservatives, he argues, these genes must have been selected for because they endowed them with some advantage. For this reason alone, we (speaking to liberals) should at the very least listen to them. Haidt has also launched a pledge at civilpolitics.org to model civility in our lives and value it as a criterion for electing candidates.

Yet another sort of tolerance movement is the so-called "coffee parties." Starting on Facebook.com, this movement encourages people to meet together over coffee to listen to and try to understand each other. I discovered it as I was writing this book and had already attempted something similar with people I knew. Although some among them would try to make them opposed to the "tea parties," claiming that those in the tea parties are the ones trying to shout down debate, I believe the two movements are complimentary. The tea parties are about getting Washington to listen to us, while the coffee parties are about us getting to listen to each other. Those in the tea parties recognize that politicians collude to divide us and the more the government controls, the more there is for us to struggle with each other over. Thus, the tea parties are as much about unity and tolerance as they are about lower taxes and smaller government.

This is the time we need true compromise, but not the variety of compromise wherein nobody gets quite what they want. This only breeds contempt and merely "buys time" while perceived injustice continues, putting off conflict for another day. What we need is the sort of lasting compromise wherein everybody gets exactly what they want. To be fair, there may be some issues on which no such compromise is possible, but far too often when such compromises are presented, they are rejected because those in power cannot afford to lose the issues of division they use in their campaign platforms.

I will give two examples. Embryonic stem cell research has great potential for generating all sorts of medical breakthroughs, but getting the stem cells requires destroying the embryos. Some see this as a form of murder. Understandably, they are against supporting such practices – even through taxes. Allowing private companies to conduct this research legally is bad enough, they reason, but the government taking money from the rest of us against our will to support such practices is much worse. Can there be an acceptable compromise? Yes. In 2001, President Bush issued the rule to restrict federal funding to creating new stem cell lines (5). Bush never stopped private sector funding. He never stopped state funding. He never stopped federal funding for research on stem cell lines already created. Since the life-or-death decision has already been made for these embryos, it made no sense to him to restrict research on the stem cell lines, which should have been able to replicate indefinitely. Bush gave both sides exactly what they said they wanted. Conservatives didn't want more people to be killed in their name with their money. Liberals wanted more research done for health improvement purposes. Everyone should have been happy. What happened?

Democrats could not afford to lose a powerful issue to use against Republicans and would never give Bush any credit for solving anything. They called Bush's order a "ban on stem cell research", when it was nothing of the sort. In the meantime, the ridiculous right criticized Bush for not doing more, inventing the questionable argument that funding any sort of stem cell research encouraged killing more embryos. Sometimes, you just can't win.

President Bill Clinton was caught in a similar trap. Patriotic homosexuals have long wanted to serve their country in the military, but many in the military were understandably concerned that there might develop certain social problems in the military subculture, possibly even damaging combat readiness and morale. President Clinton instituted the "don't ask, don't tell" policy. Homosexuals could now serve as they had always wanted, but as long as nobody discussed sexuality, nobody would know who was who. Thus, there could be no resultant social problems. Clinton gave each side what they said they wanted. Was he hailed as a hero? Of course not. Homosexual activists insisted on serving openly and the right used this issue to paint Clinton as a far left loon trying to destroy the family.

Also in this current climate, I see conspiracy theories proliferating. These feed on and feed into our fears of and distrust of government. Some distrust is healthy, to prevent opportunists from taking advantage of us, but too much distrust destroys the very foundation of society. Obviously, when my government is up to no good, I want to know about it so the problem can be dealt with, but I need real evidence. Acting without proof may hurt good people who are exactly the ones we want in government keeping an eye out for real conspiracies. Conspiracy theories are not helpful. Stay away from them and ask for solid proof.

I have several problems with every conspiracy theory I have ever heard. First, the evidence for them is usually no stronger than the evidence supporting the official version of events. While there sometimes appear to be holes in the official story, the holes in the conspiracy theory are usually larger. Second, any evidence brought against a conspiracy theory is always claimed to be yet another part of "the coverup" by authorities. When there is no way to disprove a theory even in principle, it ceases to be a theory with any merit. Third, witnesses that support the official version of events are usually dismissed because of some spurious connection to entities involved, giving them a perceived motive to contribute to the coverup. The thing is: those who spread conspiracy theories often also have something to gain. It could be as simple as wanting to make the opposing party look bad, or simply wanting to sell more books – about their conspiracy theories. On the other hand, it could be merely a distraction to hide an even larger conspiracy – or, I might think so if I were prone to such thoughts. Finally, most conspiracy theories leave me feeling powerless. To pull off a coverup of this magnitude, I reason, would take forces so powerful that I cannot even begin to think how one might discover the truth of whether this theory is correct, let alone act on it to carry out justice. Why even tell people then? It only makes them worry when they can do nothing about it.

Some people suggest that every politician is in on the same monster secret conspiracy to control us all. They believe that all politicians lie and that none of them truly believes what they run on. As for me, I am much more likely to see mere stupidity than malice. I recognize that for a politician to get elected, a sizeable number of people must believe his/her lies. It is possible that some of those followers will become the next generation of politicians. If it is possible for followers to believe, it is also possible for leaders to believe, and so it is possible that not all politicians are misleading us *deliberately*. At least, so I like to think.

Thus, I pay little attention to such ideas, but many of my friends do. This prevents us from having a reasonable discussion about moral/ political values, a subject that in many ways defines all of us in how we live our lives. That they cannot give a solid reason why they believe what they do, only serves to make me doubt their sanity. How can I eat with them, ride with them, or go into business with them with those kinds of doubts? Fortunately, their insanity seems to be only partial. Conspiracy theories, then, divide us further. Stay away from them.

Just to be clear about what I mean by conspiracy theories, not everyone labeled a conspiracy theorist deserves the label. Again, I will use Glenn Beck as an example. Beck often looks at connections between people as a clue to what they might have in mind. That SEIU leader Andy Stern has met with Obama regularly (6) and former special advisor for green jobs Van Jones was a self-described communist (7) are matters of historical record. Glenn makes no claims of conspiracy. As he says, he is "just asking questions" that any good reporter would of our elected officials. In fact, Beck makes some of the same warnings about conspiracy theories that I do, and it was Van Jones that himself was a "9-11 truther" (8). Glenn Beck may be high-strung and prone to worry, but he is no conspiracy theorist.

With current conditions as they are, including high unemployment, political turmoil, and conspiracy theories out of control, militias start to look very tempting. Again, watch out! Obviously, our constitution allows citizens to own firearms and to peaceably assemble. The states have the right to form militias for their protection. Just be careful who you're dealing with when you join. The last thing we need now is more infighting.

Perhaps worst of all is the temptation to give up trying to reach people. Sometimes people need some time to mull things over before agreeing with you. This is even harder if they first have to accept that everything they have ever been told is a lie. You don't know what people are thinking and you don't know who is hopelessly lost. Don't give up. That is how the enemies of democracy win. Democracy is impossible when the people don't communicate. But remember, while reaching out to others, stop and listen yourself. You may learn something important.

This is the time we need to communicate more, not less. This is the time we need to pull together. This is the time we need to ask all the questions we can to understand all sides of the issues. For lasting solutions, this is the time we need to start understanding each other.

# The False Choice

Suppose I were to tell you that I was a liberal. Would you think twice about buying this book? Might it be filled with nothing but Democratic propaganda under the guise of "reaching out"? Would it make you see my previous words in the first chapter under a different light? Would you reinterpret anything? What if I said I was a conservative?

Current politics in the United States is usually framed in terms of left and right. On any issue with at least two sides, those on one side are defined as conservative, those on the other as liberal, and all others as moderates. The thing is, people who take a liberal stance on one position often take a conservative stance on another and moderates are far too diverse a group to be given the single name "moderate". Some moderates are termed such because they are very conservative on some issues and very liberal on others. Other moderates are very *liberal* on some issues and very *conservative* on others (the extreme opposite of the first group). Other moderates are right in the middle on most issues, and some moderates are termed such not because of beliefs, but only because they don't strongly care about their positions.

We use these labels to divide people into those we think are reasonable and trustworthy, and those that bear watching. The use of these labels is nearly ubiquitous, and people use them to identify themselves as well as others. We seem to think these labels are important, but the truth is that they have no agreed upon meaning – which really means they have no meaning at all.

What are some of these ways in which liberalism and conservatism are defined? I list several I have heard used personally below. Some may surprise you.

**Change:** Liberals are those that enjoy trying out new things and are willing to take the risks of experimentation when it comes to improving societal institutions. Conservatives are more risk-averse and uncomfortable with change. On the flip side, they tend to think things through a little more.

This definition is of little use today. Some liberals resist changes such as President G. W. Bush's plan to partially privatize social security, while some conservatives embrace changes such as Steve Forbes's proposal for a flat tax. In my lifetime, it has been my experience that Republicans are more creative and full of ideas of how to improve things (or ruin them) while democrats cling to the same failing ideas we have been using since The New Deal, although they may offer changes in the form of slight tweaks or additions to the same paradigm.

My analysis, of course, betrays my bias of what I consider to be a "true" change, and what I consider to be yet another form of the old ways. This is the major problem with this definition; there is no agreed upon criteria for evaluating change.

**Truth:** In the waning years of the Bush administration, accusations from the left of lying, misleading, and secrecy abounded. It was in this environment that it was explicitly stated by a guest on The Daily Show that all "liberal" means is "love of the truth", whereas conservatives supposedly were less interested in the truth. One of my acquaintances later claimed, "There is no such thing as the conservative movement; there are only liars."

This definition probably isn't the best to use, because while politicians of all parties lie (even including liberal democrats), our friends, family, and strangers at the bus stop have no reason to. What do they have to gain? While the conservative ideology may indeed be based on lies, one cannot legitimately deny that there are literally millions of people that truly believe it. They have no agenda. They love the truth as much as anybody else and I hardly think that those that describe themselves as conservatives mean to advertise their disdain for the truth. Besides, in my experience, those who seem the least likely to even examine the evidence are generally apolitical, or independents.

**Money:** Under this definition, one's position on every conceivable issue derives from one simple principle: who gets the money? Liberals are at heart socialists, who want equality at all costs. They support racist affirmative action hiring programs to equalize the races, they support radical feminism to equalize the sexes, they oppose anything remotely Christian on public land to equalize the religions, and they oppose the military because all nations are equal. Everything comes back to supporting socialism (thoroughly synonymous with oppression and government theft). Conservatives, on the other hand, believe in freedom and allowing the laws of nature to dictate who gets what. The right to free speech allows conservatives to make money from publishing. The right to bear arms allows conservatives to make money by selling guns. It all comes back to capitalism (thoroughly synonymous with freedom). This definition is used implicitly by various right-wing radio talk show hosts.

The problem with this definition is that liberals are therefore inconsistent. While they loathe the use of force by the military (even to protect the homeland and therefore their socialist programs), they are perfectly happy to use force through the courts and police to ensure compliance of their fellow citizens with those same socialist programs. Radical environmentalists oppose most modern industry, including those that provide jobs to union members, yet both environmentalists and union members are considered to be in the same group – liberal. Liberals support the downtrodden when they are poor, unwed mothers-to-be, but not when they are the poor, unborn, children-to-be. This definition is therefore internally inconsistent and must be thrown out with the others. It makes no predictions of whether one will support a given proposal or not.

**Interest Groups:** "Liberal" means nothing more than the policies that result from the way in which the Democrat party is organized. Democrats promise every interest group everything it wants and then find they must break some promises when reality sets in. Conservatives insist on fairness to all from the outset, meaning some groups know they won't get everything (if they want more than what is deemed their fair share). Reality never sets in for the rank-and-file Democrats and they continue to insist on giving everybody everything they ask for. This definition is used implicitly by various right-wing radio talk show hosts.

**Constituent Relations:** Liberals believe in democracy (hence the name "Democrat"), meaning that the citizenry should govern and the elected official is purely a representative of their wishes, to vote as the public sees fit. Thus, polls are seen as a helpful tool to ensure that the representative remains informed and responsive to public opinion. Conservatives believe in republics (hence the term "Republican"), meaning they recognize that the public often does not have the education or time necessary to make complex decisions and the majority can often be wrong. Thus, conservatives respect politicians that are honest, will do what is right, and pay no attention to the shifting poll numbers of the fickle populace.

It is said that this is why Democrat politicians are more likely to make numerous promises they know they can't keep (see interest groups), which is why Democrats are more likely to elect dishonest people. Whether this is at all true or not, it fails to explain positions on a wide range of issues where liberals are in the minority (death penalty, school vouchers, gay marriage, illegal immigration) and is pretty much useless.

**Optimism 1:** Liberals are those who say, "You can't do it yourself. The system is against you. You need our help." Conservatives are those who say, "Don't give up. Everyone who has become great had to overcome some obstacle. You can do it yourself with time. Leaning on others makes you dependent." Liberals are those who say, "Climate change will kill us all! The uninsured are dying in the streets! The world will soon run out of food! We need to do something!" Conservatives are those who say, "Things are better than they used to be. The system is working. Let's wait until all the data is in before rushing to conclusions.

There's no reason to get upset yet." Liberals are pessimists and conservatives are optimists.

**Optimism 2:** Liberals are those who say, "Have some hope, we will help you get by in the meantime." Conservatives say, "Sink or swim on your own. It is good for efficiency that those doing poorly are allowed to fail." Liberals say, "Is Iraq truly a threat? Diplomacy can still work in time." Conservatives say, "Terrorists will kill us all! Secularists are trying to outlaw Christmas! We need to do something!" Liberals are optimists and conservatives are pessimists.

**Power 1:** Liberals are those that want to run every aspect of your life. Conservatism is all about freedom to do anything that doesn't infringe upon the freedom of others.

**Power 2:** Conservatives are those that want to run every aspect of your life. Liberalism is all about the freedom to do anything that doesn't infringe upon the freedom of others.

**Gender Roles:** Liberals are merely those whose maternal instincts to care for and give comfort to those less fortunate dominate.

Conservatives are merely those whose paternal instincts to instill discipline and build character dominate (9). We need both.

By this logic, one's political beliefs stem from one's attitudes toward others in everyday life. This is not the case. Some of the most unsympathetic jerks I have ever known were all for expanding social programs.

**Libertarian:** Libertarians have a completely different take on the liberal-conservative dimension. Issues are either economic (minimum wage, income taxes) or personal (the draft, drug use). Libertarians believe in all freedom, liberals believe only in personal freedom, conservatives believe only in economic freedom, and fascists believe in no freedom. Thus, there are two dimensions: one for each set of issues.

By the libertarian definitions, I know that many libertarians call themselves conservatives and many liberals call themselves libertarians. They are clearly using some other definition. This definition suffers from the fact that there is no clear division between economic and personal issues. Consider the issue of whether drug *sales* should be regulated.

In addition, it makes little sense to say that conservatives are against personal freedom when it is primarily conservatives that support gun ownership rights, and it makes little sense to say that liberals are for personal freedom when it is primarily liberals who have blocked school voucher programs – or is that an economic issue?

**3-D:** Some go further, dividing issues into social, fiscal, and foreign policy categories. Social conservatives oppose abortion and redefining marriage. Fiscal conservatives oppose excessive spending, borrowing, taxation, or currency devaluation. Foreign policy conservatives support a strong military and a diplomacy that aggressively defends American interests. One may be a liberal on one issue set and a conservative on another.

These sets need some further evaluation. Rush Limbaugh, among others, often associates conservatism with a state of military readiness and a willingness to do what is necessary to defend ourselves. He associates liberalism with pacifism. What then, is Congressman Ron Paul? Ron Paul is no pacifist. He believes in a strong military – and he is certainly no liberal. Yet Ron Paul opposed pre-emption, intervention, nation-building, long-term occupation, and just about everything the Bush Administration was involved with overseas – things that are today associated with conservatism.

Perhaps it would make more sense to divide people into several schools of thought as Joseph S. Nye Jr. has in his 2004 book Soft Power. When it comes to foreign policy, there are Jeffersonians, Hamiltonians, Jacksonians, and Wilsonians. Jeffersonians generally believe in keeping out of military conflicts while setting an example for the rest of the world in how to arrange public life. Hamiltonians generally believe in acting in America's economic interests, whatever it leads to. Jacksonians generally believe not only in defeating America's enemies, but making an example of them by using overwhelming force so that all others will think twice about messing with us. Wilsonians generally believe that only by working together with other nations to actively intervene in all minor conflicts can we avoid escalation into larger conflicts. We must make the world "safe for democracy."

Clearly, these philosophies are not mutually exclusive. One may adopt parts of each at different times. At the same time, it glosses over differences in application. Is pollution that crosses borders something a Wilsonian would consider a minor conflict? Is it better to wait on the United Nations or to assemble a "coalition of the willing?" Can a Jacksonian make an exception for those who are seeking martyrdom by easing off "making an example of them" and still consider themselves Jacksonian?

Of course, foreign policy is more than just military alliances. It includes political activity, such as the UN, the International Court of Arbitration, and human rights treaties. It also includes economics, such as duties, tariffs, NAFTA, the WTO, and the G-8. Seen in this light, the lines between liberals and conservatives begin to blur, and nobody seems to know how to classify Pat Buchannan.

Does the reasoning behind one's stances count towards classification? Sometimes they do. Those that oppose free trade on the grounds that American workers will be hurt as their jobs are outsourced overseas are often referred to as liberal. Those that oppose free trade on the grounds that it will make us dependent and therefore vulnerable to blockade during wartime are often referred to as conservative. What then, are those that support free trade? Nazis? Monarchists? Theocrats? Since the reasoning behind one's stances is often complex and misrepresented by friend and foe alike, this potentially makes every liberal a conservative and every conservative a liberal on issues from abortion to imminent domain to the capital gains tax.

Most people are not conservative, liberal, or moderate. These terms mean nothing. We may disagree more with some members of our own group than with some members of the opposing group. Yet we still use these terms as a way of marginalizing and dismissing others. In a way, these terms force us to disagree. How we interpret one's words or actions depends in part on the mindset we assume they have and on the larger political context.

Consider the statement "They're for the powerful, we're for the people." It sounds like it might have come straight from the lips of a tea party leader. Those nut jobs must be ranting against the "powerful" Democrats in congress again, you might think. I can't believe they think they represent the people, you might think. Actually, those words were spoken by Al Gore during the 2000 presidential campaign (10). The "people" to him were his constituents and the "powerful" were drug companies, insurance companies, oil companies and more. How you take something can depend on who says it.

Consider the term "military welfare". Does it refer to military personnel being used in a humanitarian aid capacity, rather than for their primary job of "killing people and breaking stuff" as Rush Limbaugh so colorfully puts it, or does it mean propping up and supporting weak, freeloading regimes that refuse to take the difficult steps necessary to defend themselves, content to let us do all the hard work? It depends who says it, but we should not jump to conclusions based on the party they belong to. It is assumptions like these that have led to many misunderstandings.

I have found in the past that people bring along a lot of baggage with them when they interpret my words. When I tried once to explain my position on homosexuality, one that is in my experience right down the middle, I was attacked for every word I typed. I commented on the debate over whether homosexuality was a sin in the Judeo-Christian tradition and was accused of taking the bible as law and endorsing theocracy (I don't). I stated that while I had nothing against it myself, I recognized that having homosexuals in the military might make *others* uncomfortable enough to impact work performance and was accused of being a bigot.

This, more than anything else in the political realm, is what frustrates me. I call myself an independent so people will have to actually listen and think to understand what I'm saying, rather than just fill in the gaps based on what they think they know about Democrat or Republican philosophy. Even then, as happened with explaining my perspective on homosexuality, I get put into boxes anyways. I once mentioned to one of my friends that presidential candidate Mike Huckabee sounded intelligent, and I was simply assumed from then on to be some sort of Christian fundamentalist. I don't even know what that means! Oddly enough, just three years earlier, another of my friends had assumed I was an atheist.

Even worse, some people go out of their way to find hidden meanings and code language imbedded in politicians' speeches. "Social justice," as the term is used, can mean many things. Democrats often use the term to speak of equal pay for equal work, ending discriminatory hiring practices, making sure that all convicted are truly guilty, and making sure that all guilty are convicted. However, it can also mean "socialism," and this is how right-wing talk show hosts generally take it. They claim it to be "doublespeak," giving one impression to one set of voters and quite a different impression to another. Those sympathetic to socialism will hear the liberal code term for socialism "social justice" and be happy. Meanwhile, those less "in the know" and less sympathetic to socialism will not be afraid. Who would be against justice?

These accusations are not helpful. Words can mean different things depending on the context and accusing the opposing party of using code words will only make the accusers look paranoid and silly. Whether "social justice" began as a code word is irrelevant. After being used so many times to refer to things other than socialism, non-socialists may very well have picked up on the term and started using it. To accuse these people of also being socialists only brings conflict and further unnecessary division. It would make more sense to actually listen to what candidates say and scrutinize their records than to search for alternative meanings to some isolated phrases.

To be fair, the left generates its fair share of accusations too. Republican candidates for president are often asked if they would have a "litmus test" on abortion for choosing Supreme Court justices. These candidates often respond by saying that they will choose justices that "interpret the law as written and will not legislate from the bench." This sounds fair enough. After all, to do otherwise would violate the principle of separate, co-equal branches of government. According to left-wing political analysts, however, this is code for taking away abortion rights.

This is why we don't listen to each other anymore. Instead of taking what people mean, we assume they are regurgitating talking points from the other side. Somebody pleads for helping the poor and all we hear is "sack the rich and middle-class to support an intrusive, bloated bureaucracy – and maybe help the poor along the way." Somebody pleads for setting some measurable goals and standards in our war efforts by which to judge whether we are conducting the war in the right way and all we hear is "we surrender!" Somebody pleads for us to do something about racism in this country and all we hear is "take jobs from light-skinned people and give them to others, regardless of talent." Welfare, timetables, affirmative action, separation of church and state, fiscal responsibility, family values, civil liberties, privacy rights, states' rights, multilateralism – these are all accused of being code terms for something other than they are. Is it any wonder we so distrust politicians? Is it any wonder that we don't understand each other?

Talk show hosts across the political spectrum are quick to assume the worst of people and interpret their words in bad light. Director of National Intelligence Dennis Blair, when speaking of the underwear bomber and preventing terrorism in general, said, "We won't make that mistake again; we'll make a new one."(11) This is a statement that is impossible to argue with. Mistakes are an inevitable part of life. If he had said that we would never make another mistake, he would have been accused of arrogance. Mr. Blair was merely being realistic and honest. Of course, this statement quickly became a right-wing talking point used to paint the entire Obama administration as not taking terrorism seriously.

Also, as a presidential candidate, Barack Obama was once heard suggesting that we properly inflate our tires to increase fuel efficiency as part of a means to cope with high gas prices. This is not a bad idea, though the difference it makes overall is of course miniscule. Ann Coulter was quick to pick up on this, sarcastically suggesting that to solve the health care cost crisis, everyone should eat an apple a day(12). This is not a bad idea either, but Ann used it to make Obama look inept and foolish, as if properly inflated tires were the entirety of his plan. Why are we all so quick to assume the worst of people?

It is the media that brings these statements to our attention and the media that interprets them for us. Unfortunately, we aren't all listening to the same people. Chris Matthews and Keith Olbermann paint a very different picture of reality than Sean Hannity. The Confederate Flag represents slavery to some people and a state's freedom from federal intrusion to others (in many ways, the opposite of slavery). We should discuss our impressions and fill each other in on gaps in our worldviews, but instead we avoid each other. Few of us are willing to talk to the nutcase across the street, and few of those nutcases are willing to talk to us. It is the media that uses terms like "conservative" and "liberal" to divide us, but if we took the time to understand each other, we might find we have more in common than we think.

I have wondered for years whether these groups (liberal, conservative, and moderate) even exist. Of course, I always knew there were lots of people that didn't fit in, but I could never be sure whether or not most people did. Surely, for the terms to continue to be used, there must be some real pattern amongst all the noise – right? No. Without the resources to launch my own study, I instead combed through old books and databases for previous work on the subject. Finally, in the 1973 book <u>Measures of Political Attitudes</u> by John

P. Robinson, Jerrold G. Rush, and Kendra B. Head, I found the following quote on page thirty-five:

"Terms like 'liberalism' and 'conservatism' have had little meaning to most voters; only minorities have defined these terms with regards to politics, which suggests the lack of an all-embracing ideological structure or frame of reference within which specific issues and events are viewed. Many people indicate no preference between generally 'liberal' and 'conservative' policies or candidates when such questions have been posed."

On page seventy-nine is an even clearer quote:

"The liberal-conservative dimension has intrigued scholars for years with its potential for explaining the variation in political attitudes of the populace. However, these hopes faded when encountered with research done on a mass level. Repeated samples of the mass electorate by the Survey Research Center (Campbell et al, 1960; Converse, 1964) have convincingly demonstrated that no such organizing dimension or ideological structure exists for most citizens. Correlations between specific issue items were often low and when such congruence occurred, it was generally for other reasons than that of ideology (i.e., most usually a result of self-interest or group preference)."

As early as 1973 it was known that these terms meant next-to-nothing. Why do we still continue to use them? Has anything changed since then? If we have become more polarized, is it possible that this is the effect of using these terms – a sort of self-fulfilling prophecy? Psychologists have known for years about such phenomena as groupthink, confirmation biases, attachment, stigmatization, internalization, and patternicity (thank you, Michael Shermer). Any one of these could explain our growing polarization. Could the media even be doing this on purpose? I don't know.

What I do know is that the media creates issues for us to debate – almost out of thin air. Do you remember how our ongoing subsidies to farmers in violation of WTO (World Trade Organization) rules were a big issue of discussion during the last presidential election? No? You don't? What about health care? Yes? Why was health care such a big issue? Was there truly a groundswell of interest by the electorate that the media couldn't ignore? If so, how did the electorate realize there was a problem I wonder? If some of them personally felt the brunt of rising costs, what made them think of it in terms of a widespread problem rather than a personal one? What made them think of it in terms of a problem for government to fix rather than churches, charities, schools, science, or business? Was affordable access to health care truly a bigger problem than global warming, warring Mexican drug lords on our border, and our subsidies to farmers? (13) If the media had focused instead on these issues in the years before the election, might we possibly have ignored health care? The media control it all and they all copy each other.

The media tends to focus more heavily on those issues that divide us the most. Perhaps this is for ratings. Perhaps this for no other reason than that it would be a waste of time to discuss issues on which we are all in agreement. I don't know, but focusing on only a few, highly divisive issues creates the impression that there are two distinct groups of us, defined as liberals and conservatives. Don't let them fool you. If they brought in more issues to discuss, the group designations would dissolve as there would be as much disagreement within groups as between them. Your enemy today may be your enemy's enemy tomorrow, and as the saying goes, the enemy of your enemy is your friend.

# More Alike Than You Think

I have for years wondered whether my disagreements with others were truly as deep as they seemed. I have, on occasion, been able to continue a debate long enough to realize that I was arguing semantics. It seems that there are many words that mean different things to different people, especially in the realms of politics, philosophy, and religion. This makes things very confusing.

I tend to think of myself as a capitalist. That is, I believe that so long as I'm not hurting anyone, it is nobody's business but mine (and especially not the government's) what I do with my own stuff. To me, communism is when the government goes through my bank account, takes whatever they want, and spends it how they choose. In a democracy, the government is made up of our fellow citizens. Would you let them go through your bank account? Would you let *me* go through your bank account? This is communism.

Imagine my surprise when one of my coworkers mentioned she was a communist. Luckily, I had enough rapport with her that we were able to debate without arguing. After listening a while, I realized she wasn't talking about the same thing. While I speak in the language of state policy and economic systems, she speaks in the language of cultural values and attitudes. To me, capitalism is about freedom, independence, and individuality. To her, capitalism is about materialism, selfishness, greed, mindless competition, division, and callousness. To me, communism is tyranny and theft. To her, it is when people respect and care for each other. It is generosity and unity. In those terms, I'm a communist too. To my relief, she has no plans to overthrow the government.

I suspect that if we actually took the time to listen to each other's concerns, we would find we have a lot in common. Liberal, moderate, libertarian, and conservative mean nothing. We are all individuals. Below, I have compiled a list of some other words taken in different ways by different people.

**Capitalism:** To many people, capitalism is the economic system wherein one is free to buy, sell, save, invest, and otherwise enjoy all one's assets, free from interference from the government, organized crime, or anybody else. By differences in education, talent, drive, and pure luck, some people may do better than others. Some of the better off may choose to be generous. Some of the better off may choose to be callous. All types are accepted, and no one can decide for another how much to give – or in what form. Even local communes are free to exist in a capitalist society. It is all about freedom. Capitalism is represented by those who made it big starting from scratch, like Steve Jobs and Henry Ford.

To many other people, capitalism is the competitive drive to outdo everybody else at all costs, including fraud, theft, stock market manipulation, slander, libel, intimidation, collusion, destroying the natural world, and compromising safety. The ultimate goal is to make more money. Anyone that doesn't play along is subjugated. Capitalism is represented by those who sacrificed ethics to serve money, like Bernie Madoff and Kenneth Lay.

Before you debate capitalism, make sure you are debating about the same thing.

**Communism:** To many people, communism is the economic system wherein every aspect of life is regulated, implicitly or explicitly, by the state. Without the right to enjoy the fruits of one's labor, one is instead enticed to work by the threat of force. The bureaucracy creates one-size-fits-all standards to treat everyone, not as individuals with different needs and talents, but as expendable automatons to serve the collective. Communism is represented by harsh tyrannies such as North Korea and the Former Soviet Union.

To many other people, communism is the state in which many hunter-gatherer groups live, sharing the common bounties of the band or tribe. Everyone has value, and so everyone is cared for. Knowing that they will be taken care of by the others in times of trouble, every member is more than happy to help the group when they can. Communism is represented by loving families, some churches, and hippie communes.

Before you debate communism, make sure you are debating about the same thing.

**Fairness:** To some people, fairness is when everyone is equally free from government interference, able to succeed or fail afterwards. To other people, fairness is when people are also equally free from prejudicial discrimination, able to succeed or fail on merit. To other people, fairness is when everyone is given the same level of education, able to succeed or fail based on their level of determination. To still others, fairness is only when everyone succeeds or fails equally together. Some people see the lottery as fair, because everyone that participates has an equal chance of winning, even though only one person actually wins. Others think of the lottery as fair because it is voluntary. Others think of it as unfair, because not everyone wins. Others think of the lottery as unfair because the amount won is not proportional to the number of tickets bought by that individual.

Some people think of fair more in terms of making sure those who do wrong are punished. Some people think of fair more in terms of making sure those who do right are rewarded. To them, it is unfair to not be rewarded for doing well. Finally, some think of fair more in terms of making sure those who do wrong are *not* rewarded and those who do right are *not* punished. The next time you hear somebody describe a situation as fair or unfair, consider this paragraph.

**Born-Again Christian:** Some people think of a born-again Christian as one who converts later in life, as opposed to one raised in a Christian household. Other people think of a born-again Christian as a member of a specific sect – usually Charismatic or Pentecostal. Finally, many people speak of "born-again" in the same way the bible does. To become a Christian, one must accept Jesus into their heart, accept that they have been forgiven for their sins, and hence become "spiritually" reborn. To them, a born-again

Christian is a redundant term. The next time a candidate for political office is described as a born-again Christian, don't assume you know what this means. They are not all alike.

**Marriage:** To many people, a marriage is a special type of loving relationship and partnership between two people. It does not include parent-child relationships, standard friendships, or business partnerships. However, it may be comprised of any two people regardless of sex, and it is possible to be married to more than one person at the same time.

To other people, marriage is an even more special relationship and partnership that is monogamous, permanent (till death), and inherently heterosexual. One partner fills the husband role (male) and the other fills the wife role (female). To those who have experienced romantic love, they know first-hand of its inherently monogamous, permanent, and heterosexual nature. To think of it otherwise is nonsensical and an insult to their deepest feelings.

If you are of the first group, understand that most people are never going to call your relationship by the same name as theirs. Different types of things deserve different names – to avoid confusion. Remember, unless you have experienced romantic, heterosexual love, you won't be in a position to know of its fundamentally distinct nature.

If you are of the second group, the next time you hear of homosexuality activists pushing for your state to recognize "gay marriage", understand that they don't mean it the same way you do. They aren't trying to undermine the family or make a mockery of your love and institutions; they don't know any better.

If any debate in this country could use more dialogue and tolerance, it is this one. Holding signs that say, "God hates fags," is hardly fostering respect and understanding any more than homosexuals that flaunt their sexuality in public. For the record, I support civil unions. I believe that if you aren't married you should be able to officially designate a partner to handle your finances, share your accounts, file your taxes with, buy insurance with, and visit you in the hospital. Straights should be able to get civil unions too. What you may or may not do or have done in the bedroom is absolutely none of my business – and frankly, I don't want it to be. Keep it to yourself. Understand, though, that this is not marriage by the definition I grew up with.

**Faith:** Listening to self-described atheists, one gets the picture that faith is when one stubbornly clings to old, sometimes ridiculous ideas indefinitely when they are contradicted by evidence. Obviously, this is the type of faith we could do with less of. It is synonymous with close-mindedness and delusion. On the other hand, the faithful describe faith as synonymous with trust. No one will deny that trust may sometimes be misplaced, but most will argue that without trust there is nothing. When we drive over a bridge, we put our trust in the skill of the engineers, and the fact that since the bridge held the last time we drove over it, it will most likely do so again. When we deposit money in the bank, we trust that we can retrieve it later. When we buy food at the store, we trust it is not contaminated with botulism. Trust may sometimes be tested by new reports, but in a healthy, trusting relationship, one does not withdraw immediately, but instead weighs the evidence carefully on both sides for a time and waits to see if more reports arise that refute the first report. Those who continually change their minds are unstable and don't get very far with anything. By this second definition, faith is not opposed to reason, but is complimentary to it.

Remember, the next time you meet people who rigidly stick with their religious beliefs, don't criticize them for having faith; they may know something you don't, you may know something they don't, or possibly both. Remember, the next time you find people that believe in evolutionary theory despite your most eloquent arguments against it, they aren't going to change their minds overnight. Proper faith in evolutionary theory dictates that one should be slow and careful to examine the totality of the evidence before giving up such a lifelong belief. Remember, the next time you meet lifelong Democrats, pointing out a single ridiculous comment by Nancy Pelosi will not convince them to switch. Remember, the next time you meet lifelong Republicans, pointing out one misstatement by Dick Cheney will not convince them to switch. This is faith. Everyone has faith in something.

The next time one is accused of being faithless or faithful, ask what it means.

**Liar:** A liar is one who spreads lies (false statements). This is the definition used by some claiming President G. W. Bush lied about there being WMDs in Iraq. However, to most, a liar is not one who merely repeats lies, but one who creates lies and so spreads them *purposefully*. At least some of those calling Bush a liar will admit he didn't know any better (14). The fact that they willingly admit that Bush might have actually believed what he said while still calling him a liar proves that they are not merely involved in a smear campaign. Clearly, this is a different definition that has caused much confusion and needless animosity.

**Racists:** To some, racists are not merely those who harbor hate for or prejudicial beliefs about members of various races, but those that also have the power to act on those beliefs. Racism is more about behavior than thoughts. Speaking not of individuals, but of races, American whites are racist, while American Blacks are not – because whites tend to have more power in America however you measure it. So racism is a large-scale, sociological phenomenon, and not something that happens at the personal level between individuals.

Other people make no distinction between discrimination based on race and discrimination based on cultural behaviors. Since there exist practices accepted in some cultures that are hated most everywhere else, this makes most people at least somewhat racist by this definition.

**Rights:** The word "rights" is used in different ways depending on the context. It can mean guarantees made by the state, such as a right to an attorney and due process. There is another way the word is used also. It can also mean those things that are no one else's business to regulate (not even the government's), such as the right to peaceably assemble, the right to bear arms, and the right to free speech. Some call these God-given rights.

Conservatives and liberals conceptualize God-given rights very differently. Liberals recognize that more freedom to some means less to others and they must balance these rights against each other. There are trade-offs. So while they recognize a right of association of the employer to fire anybody for any reason, they also recognize the right of the employee to a job. After weighing the pros and cons, they decide which right to support. Rights, therefore, are anything that would be good for somebody.

Though it may be a surprise to liberals, conservatives are also keenly aware of these trade-offs, but they only label those things as "rights" that survive the cost-benefit analysis. To conservatives, there is no "right" to a job, because the right of association takes precedence. Liberals label first and do the math after. Conservatives do the math first and label after.

To a conservative, a "right" to health care is utter nonsense. Unlike free speech, which only requires that one be allowed to speak without interference and doesn't require anything of anyone else (It doesn't even require that others listen), health care requires work on the part of health care providers, and usually somebody has to pay for materials. A "right to health care" is akin to a "right to have slaves" or a "right to violate others' rights," which would make all God-given rights meaningless.

It is the conservative conceptualization I grew up with and I thought for years that liberals were literally insane and might need to be locked up before they hurt anyone. It was only in 2010 that I found a liberal blogger who was able to explain all this to me. Liberals need to do a better job of explaining what they mean by the term "rights." Better yet, use a different term entirely – such as "interests".

With all these different definitions, it is no wonder we can't get along. If we stopped for a moment to discuss what we meant, might we discover we actually agree? Even if we don't agree, having a firmer understanding of the other person's interests will make it much easier to negotiate a compromise. For a long time, I've thought of inviting people I knew one at a time to sit down with me for coffee and explain how they came to believe what they believe. I wanted to understand people better. I wanted to know where they got their information, and what influences they had growing up and developing their beliefs, instincts, and biases. I thought that not only might we get along better, but that I would know better how to present my own ideas so that others would understand them. I also thought that my experiences could inspire and guide others how to undertake similar projects.

I think this is the only way out of our current mess. Our opponents don't listen to us because we don't listen to them. Meanwhile, the political class pits us against each other to win elections and continue taking advantage of all of us – and we just blame each other! It's time to start working together instead.

In my family and workplace, people are very free with political opinions. Since people seem to love to talk about themselves so much, I was surprised when few agreed to talk to me and even fewer had the patience to finish. In the beginning, there were even some misunderstandings over the aims of my project. One woman thought it was a sort of test to see how informed she was on current affairs. I scaled back my project somewhat, streamlining it to include a simple conversation of one, single issue and some follow-up questions on how they first became exposed to some of the underlying, component concepts. I wanted to explore not only the avenues through which the surface beliefs spread (such as accusations of racism), but how people come to deem one group as a reliable source of information, and another the enemy. I wanted to understand differences I had observed in how evidence is approached and the fundamental axiomatic assumptions upon which all other thinking is based. Still, I was frustrated.

One man talked in circles with me. Every time I thought progress was made explaining how my natural aversion to open homosexuality was in no way "pre-judging" those who identify themselves as homosexuals of having any other stereotypical characteristics, he continued to state that my position was prejudiced. I asked what it was that made it sound that way, but he would not identify anything.

One woman I found could be convinced of anything. She only repeats what she hears. She is a Republican because her husband is, but the social programs she supports put her to the economic left of some Democrats. By the end of our session, I had easily convinced her that price controls constituted an invasion of privacy, caused economic harm, and were related to communistic thinking. I never was able to find out where she gets a lot of her ideas.

Finally, I started a blog at TheUnderstanding Project.com where I explained to the best of my ability what the different political schools of thought were. Still, I had more questions than answers. I visited other blogs I could find and asked questions and pointed things out. I've learned a lot, but I'm unsure if any have learned from me. Still, if it works for you, I encourage you to try reaching out and asking questions. Visit my blog and share your stories. Start your own blog. Most of all, lend this book to someone you know – or buy one as a Christmas present (I make more money the latter way – hint, hint).

# Media Effects

What one thing, more than anything else, drives conflict? I suspect it is the media. The media loves conflict and presents everything within that framework. Consider when Senator John McCain made his "hundred years war" comment (15). Speaking of how long we might have troops still in Iraq, John stated that we might very well station a permanent base there for deterrence as we have on the Korean peninsula. In this description, he mentioned that we might be in Iraq for a hundred years. I knew what John was talking about when he said it. I knew what he meant. I knew he didn't mean that he actually *intended* for us to be there that long, let alone continue hostilities for that long, yet the pundits in the media portrayed it this way.

In the meantime, then-Senator Barack Obama responded to his comments, making it clear to his supporters, who tended to be more anti-war, that we would not be continuing hostilities indefinitely, but must instead bring the war to a swift close. Obama never promised to pull out before we had finished our objectives, but wanted to illustrate a difference in emphasis between him and McCain. I understood what he was talking about. I knew what he meant. He was showing that it was *important* to him to end the war soon. I knew he never meant to suggest that McCain actually thought hostilities would last that long (hostilities were already well on their way down by this time), yet that is how the pundits in the media portrayed it.

While John and Barack disagreed on many topics, this was one on which they merely made different points of emphasis. The media, however, turned the whole thing into a virtual scandal, half of them claiming that Obama had twisted McCain's words dishonestly, and half of them claiming that McCain had actually intended to keep us fighting for a hundred years.

Our worldviews are the products of every bit of information we absorb. Our parents, teachers, clergy, and peers all have their influence long before we begin to listen to Michael Moore and Michelle Malkin. It is not enough to get everyone to listen to the same political analysts to agree. Who one chooses to listen to, who one deems a reliable source of information, how data is processed, and the way evidence is approached are the more important issues.

Psychologists have long known that the way people react to information depends in part on the information they have been previously fed. Mere words and images can alter moods – even outside of awareness. Giving one a test containing the words "Florida" and "wrinkle" beforehand increase the likelihood that one will walk slower than average afterward (16). In the same way, I suspect, people with certain life experiences are predisposed to be more receptive to certain arguments than others. Likewise, one who watches the television series The Rockford Files will be more receptive to news stories that portray the police negatively, whereas one who watches Chips will not. Every little thing can affect us. One may grow up seeing a Listerine commercial featuring a bottle swinging through the jungle on vines and conclude that jungles are generally full of swingable vines. One may see an episode of Family Matters wherein Harriette tells Carl that it's dangerous to wake a sleepwalker, and take this as fact. One may hear the joke contrasting the Mafia and the government (one is organized), and come away with the impression that it is a common impression that the government is generally incompetent. Does the cartoon Captain Planet make children more likely to grow up into environmentalists? This might be a phenomenon worthy of more study.

The news media covers isolated stories without historical context or future analysis. Sometimes they give a biased picture, sometimes they miss things, and they're almost always boring. This is why people like me turn to opinion shows like Rush Limbaugh and Glenn Beck. Of course I know they're biased, but at least they report on things I care about and explain them in terms I can understand. Rather than simply reporting on isolated cases, they compare and contrast long-term trends. While the news simply reports the number of years and number of casualties in Iraq, Rush will also report on how long we occupied Germany after World War Two, and the number of casualties in the United States (due to murder, car accidents, et cetera). This gives a deeper perspective that most in the mainstream media do not.

I can't trust the media. I wish I could do my own research, reading up on what the bills debated in congress really say, and interviewing experts to determine their long-term effects, but this is impossible. I work full time. The Patriot Act is longer than most books. Besides, most of those bills are written in convoluted legalese, and a lot of them don't end up passing. Can you really afford to read both the house and senate versions of the health care bill when neither might pass? Also, C-Span is boring as hell. I almost think they make it that way deliberately so no one will pay attention to how our money is spent.

Access is limited, too. I tried searching WhiteHouse.gov for information on Ken

Feinberg's job description. I wanted to see what his actual powers were and the wording of the charter that created his department. The Republicans call him a "pay czar" and make him sound spooky and dangerous. I don't want to trust Republicans, but this time I have no choice. I can't find anything on him beyond some very vaguely-worded ideals put forth by Tim Geithner when he introduced him. Not only do I not know where to go to search for information, I don't even know who to ask that might know, nor do I know who might tell me who to ask. If I distrust the Obama administration and turn to the Republicans for answers, it is his own fault for not making things more clear.

Of course, the law that passes might not be the law the public sees. It depends who the public listens to. Obama has been accused of lying about the very content of the legislation being debated (courtesy of Joe Wilson). When the president's word cannot be trusted, can we trust any posting the government puts out? Is a written statement any more trustworthy than a verbal one? Fox

News has also been accused of lying about the content of the legislation being discussed. What makes them any less (or more) trustworthy than Obama? I don't know who to believe sometimes. When you can't trust the media or the officials in government, who can you trust? Anarchists? Ouija boards? Stephen Colbert?!?

Sometimes a member of a legislature might not vote for a good bill because they are holding out for a better one already in the works. This is rarely the story that gets reported. Usually all that is mentioned is how they voted against a good bill. Voting records are not detailed enough to give the type of information necessary to judge those running for office. Sometimes, otherwise good bills are tainted by very bad provisions (often referred to as "poison pills"). Sometimes these are even snuck in on purpose (I have been told) so an opponent will be seen voting against a good bill, or so one will have an excuse to vote against a bill they secretly didn't want to pass anyways. Whether these rumors are true is not important. The very fact that we hurl these rumors at each other promotes an atmosphere of dirty tricks and incivility.

All this could be avoided if the media were more thorough and less partisan, but that won't happen any time soon. This is why I wish people listened to each other more, to fill each other in on things they might have missed.

# The Case For A Third Party

It is not only the media that divides us, but parties. In his farewell address, President George Washington warned us against entangling alliances. He recognized that an ally with common principles and interests today may not share them tomorrow. It is the classical Faustian bargain: do you continue to support your party as it betrays your deepest principles so that it might serve you better in the long run by perhaps defeating the opposing party? Parties lead people to give loyalty to the party rather than to the principles. Over time this can lead to partisanship and corruption.

I've never liked parties. They almost force people to disagree when they might not otherwise. It seems that many people feel obligated to defend their leaders against any who threaten their good standing. I've always been an independent, but even I was so disgusted by the Democrats constantly lying about George W. Bush that I eventually found myself continuing to make excuses for him even when I began to suspect that some of the lies were actually true. When confronted with Bush quotes that made him sound dangerous, I used my imagination to think of other things he might have meant. When confronted with tales of minor corruption and incompetence, I looked for any reason to believe that the higher-level administrators were not involved. I notice that this is the same type of partisan/loyalist behavior that Democrats engage in. People are much more likely to believe rumors that fit with what they already think they know than they are to accept new information that runs counter to it. My love affair with the Republicans is now over, but if the Democrats don't shape up, it won't make any difference.

The two-party system doesn't serve me very well. On the one hand, Democrats continually increase the centralization and intrusive nature of our government, regulating more and more. This might not be such a problem if the government could not muster the power to enforce these regulations – but that's where the Republicans come in. Republicans like to project the image of being tough on crime and upholding the rule of law. As part of this, they add measures that make it easier to find and apprehend those who break the law. To be sure, there are dangerous criminals that need to be caught, and Republicans may generally be responsible enough to be trusted – but the same measures used to catch bad people can be misused by future *Democrat* administrators to catch good people. No institution should have that much power! Likewise, some activities do need to be regulated, and Democrats may generally be bright enough to know how and what, and set policy accordingly – but the same regulatory agencies used for good may be misused by future *Republican* administrators. In this way, the parties work together to gradually bring us ever closer to tyranny. One does not need to erect an entire tyranny oneself when the opposing party will do half the work and receive all the blame. The two-party system leaves us with no third option and so only serves the interests of the power-hungry elites.

In any election cycle, the winning party often wins based on promises not to continue the excesses of the ruling party. To be fair, they often follow through on these promises, but do they ever repeal anything? Do they ever reverse anything? The Federal Government seems to only increase in size and expenditures. Do those leading your preferred party truly share your interests or do they secretly like the new powers the other party has created? After all, the more power the other party grabs, the easier it is to win on a platform of promising to end these types of power grabs, and then inheriting all that power oneself. Consider: Obama failed to close Guantanamo in a timely manner. The Democrats continue to fund our efforts in Iraq and Afghanistan. Bush failed to partially privatize Social Security – even when his own party controlled congress. There is little incentive to be good. When the opposing party is perceived to be awful, one merely needs to be less bad.

At this point, I may begin to sound like a conspiracy theorist – the type of people I warned you about in the first chapter, but this is different. I make no claim that leaders of both parties have met together and explicitly discussed this plan. I have no evidence to support that. Indeed, the phenomenon I describe could have happened purely by accident – or as a result of poorly understood, large-scale, social forces. What I'm saying is: if *I* was able to perceive the pattern and the benefits to those in power to continue "playing the game", so surely must have those in power – and at least some of them must now be playing deliberately, whether they have discussed it amongst themselves or not.

The only way we can get out of this mess is to have a viable third party. The more parties we have, the more likely there can be an upset, and therefore the more incentive each party has to behave to prevent that. Competition is good. It works in the marketplace. Look, I'm not saying that both parties are equally bad. In fact, I myself have a preference. What I'm saying is that the two-party system itself is flawed and becoming ever more dangerous.

The parties collude in other ways as well. Both parties are heavily involved in currency devaluation. The Fed has been monetizing the debt (17). Federal Reserve Chairman Bernanke was appointed first by Bush and later by Obama. Majorities of both parties voted to confirm him(18). Both parties passed NAFTA (19). Both parties support at least some military interventionism. Bush got us into Afghanistan and Iraq. Clinton got us into Bosnia and Kosovo, not to mention ordering missiles fired into Sudan. Both parties are heavily involved in gerrymandering districts, redrawing district boundaries with an eye to demographics to make it harder to unseat incumbents (20). Both parties are up to their eyeballs in corporate donations and lobbyists. Both parties are riddled with corruption. Democrats love to point out with glee Jack Abramoff, the lobbyist who for years ran an overbilling scam and had close ties to over one hundred Republican congressmen (21), but the Democrats have ACORN, an organization involved in so many different illegal activities (22) I could devote a whole chapter to them! If you oppose NAFTA, are you being served? If you are a pacifist, are you being served? If you dislike corruption, are you being served? True, there are differences between the parties, but that isn't enough. We deserve another choice.

Why then don't we have a third party? Actually, we have several: the libertarians, the greens, the socialists, the reform party, the natural law party, the constitution party, and others. Yet none of them does well. Are the dominant two parties really so much more popular? Why do so many vote for Republicans and Democrats? I can't speak for everybody, but I have often found myself in the position of being made so afraid of one candidate, that I felt had to defeat them at all costs. Knowing that the candidate receiving the most votes generally wins (ignore the electoral college and what happens with pluralities for the moment), and not wanting to allow the "anti-" vote to be split among several parties, I always vote for the candidate with the greatest chance of defeating the candidate I don't like – in other words, the one most of the others are voting for.

From what I have heard, this is the same problem plaguing many others. They speak of worrying they are "throwing their vote away" if they vote for a party other than the dominant two. In other words, many of us vote for the dominant parties primarily because the rest of us do. Might we not also vote for another party if we thought that more people were going to also? They vote because of how we vote and we vote because of how they vote. This is crazy. How many actually vote for who they want? Is there any way out of this dilemma? Without knowing how others are going to vote, we will never be free from the fear of losing big. Is there another way?

There has already been a system invented for dealing with just this sort of problem. It is called Condorcet voting. Under such a system, one's second, third, and sometimes further choices are counted as well as their first. In this way, preferences among the populace between every combination of two candidates are added up. Why should one give up the right to vote on the race between the Greens and Libertarians simply by voting on the race between the Greens and the Democrats? Your vote will never be "thrown away", and so there is nothing to fear by voting for who you truly like. This is what we need to institute at all levels of government in every election, to respect often neglected points of view. This is the only way to have a fair shot at ending this madness. Condorcet elections are an absolute must if we wish to end our practice of voting for "the lesser of two evils."

Other measures that have been proposed include lowering the number of signatures necessary to get someone on the ballot, thereby boosting name recognition. Term limits have also been proposed to solve a multitude of ills I won't go into here, but they will also aid third parties trying to make inroads. Incumbents are hard to unseat, but term limits would open those seats up. The media is perhaps the biggest obstacle to third parties. They claim that candidates low in the polls have no chance of winning, so why put them on? But the reason these candidates remain low in the polls is often in part because the media doesn't cover them, and so few know who they are. This creates a feedback loop, keeping the dominant parties on top. Some in the media even claim that voters can't mentally handle more than two or three choices, but the media will often set up debates with nine or more during primaries! Do the same during the general election, that's all I ask. Personally, I would like to see just the top seven.

How might we get these measures through, if any? The major parties certainly won't help us. Could we form a coalition of every minor party, united around a few core principles, and running on a platform of ballot reform, term limits, and Condorcet elections, hoping to break through and win in one, big, united campaign? It's possible. Another option is to create a pledge. Candidates signing the pledge agree to do their utmost to enact each of the measures listed. Whatever is done, now is the time to do it. Anger with the Democrats and Republicans is at an all time high.

Forty percent of those registered to vote are now independents (23).

If we do form a coalition party, can we agree enough on core principles to make it work? This I don't know. Compromise may be in order. In any case, the first step towards working together is listening.

# More About The Understanding Project

If you are looking for a place to understand and be understood, my blog, TheUnderstandingProject.com, is a good place to start. I not only post about things I learn, but about things that continue to confuse and frustrate me so you may leave comments to explain them. When I first set out on this venture, I pictured myself conducting more interviews. Instead, I have done very few. Things haven't gone entirely as planned. Most of what I have learned has come from reading the blogs of others.

I have found that when people fail to understand the motives behind one's actions, rumors tend to spread. It is rumored that those who are pro-life want to impose their religion on the rest of us. It is rumored that those against "gay rights" are insecure about their own sexuality and are overcompensating. It is rumored that the true motive behind environmentalism is to destroy capitalism by overregulation. Are any of these rumors true? The only way to know is by talking to each other.

At TheUnderstandingProject.com, I expose what arguments the common person actually makes.

Since starting my blog in the spring of 2010, I have learned many things. I have learned that there are people that actually endorse the use of labels I find misleading and divisive, such as "conservative" and "liberal." I still don't know why. I have also learned that the term "right to die" is not always about assisted suicide. Sometimes it is merely about the right to be allowed to die naturally with family and some dignity, than to be strapped to intrusive, torturous machines, which will only prolong "life" by a small amount anyways. I have also learned that in setting the record straight that carbon dioxide isn't poisonous, one will likely be misunderstood that one doesn't realize that carbon dioxide's greenhouse gas properties are more important.

Also on my blog, sometimes I suggest compromises that I think will work (at least until politics gets in the way as it did with stem cells and "don't ask, don't tell"). So far, I've covered Wikileaks and the use of torture.

It is said that many hands make work light, and so I invite anyone with the time to do so to start their own blog and link to mine. Together, we can learn so much more. I will report on what you're up to in my own blog, as I report on anything relevant to progress in political understanding. I want to build a network of similar blogs, all linked together. So start one up, and don't forget to invite the nutcase across the street.

# Endnotes

1.    Dear AIG, I Quit! Glenn Beck, 25/March/2009, 12:21 ET, http://www.glennbeck.com/content/articles/article/198/23191

2.    Raw Data Joseph Stack Suicide Manifesto, FoxNews.com, 18/February/2010, http://www.foxnews.com/us/2010/02/18/raw-data-joseph-stack-suicide-manifesto

3.    Address To Congress, President Bush, 21/September/2001, http://www.articles.cnn.com/2001-09-20/us/gen.bush.transcript_1_joint-session-national-anthem-citizens/5?_S=PM:US

4.    Cyber Alerts, vol. 5, no. 231, 6/November/2000, http://www.mediaresearch.org/cyberalerts/2000/cyb20001106_extra.asp#1

5.    Marc Sandalow, Bush Approves Strict Rules For Stem Cell Funding/ President

Rejects Call For Broader Federal Support Of
Human Embryo Research, SFGate,
10/August/2001,
http://www.articles.sfgate.com/2001-08-
10/news/17611726_1_fundamental-moral-
line-stem-cell-cell-lines

6.      Susan Davis, SEIU's Andy Stern Tops
White House Visitor List, WSJ,
30/October/2009,
http://www.blogs.wsj.com/washwire/2009/1
0/30/seius-stern-tops-white-house-visitor-list

7.      Eliza Stickland, The New Face Of
Environmentalism, East Bay Express,
2/November/2005,
http://www.eastbayexpress.com/gyrobase/t
he-new-face-of-
environmentalism/content?oid=1079539&sh
owfulltext=true

8.      Amanda Carpenter, Green Jobs Czar
Signed 'Truther' Statement In 2004,
Washington Times, 3/September/2009,
http://www.washingtontimes.com/weblogs/

back-story/2009/sep/03/green-jobs-czar-signed-truther-statement-in-2004

9.   George Lakoff, Moral Politics, http://www.press.uchicago.edu/misc/chicago/467716.html

10.   Al Gore's Nomination Acceptance Speech, http://www.acedemic.csuohio.edu/kneuendorf/content/cpuca/gorespch.htm

11.   Intel Chief Admits To Dropping Ball On Christmas Plot, 'New Mistake' Inevitable, FoxNews.com, 20/January/2010, http://www.foxnews.com/politics/2010/01/20/congress-presses-details-administrations-counterterror-policies

12.   Hannity And Colmes, 6/August/2008, http://www.foxnews.com/story/0,2933,398722,00.html

13.   Brazil Files Another WTO Complaint Against US Over Farm Subsidies, Global Subsidies Initiative, http://www.globalsubsidies.org/en/subsidy-

watch/news/brazil-files-another-wto-complaint-against-us-over-farm-subsidies

14.  Moore: Bush 'Didn't Tell The Truth', O'Reilly Factor, 27/July/2004, http://www.foxnews.com/story/0,2933,1272 36,00.html

15.  David Corn, McCain In NH: Would Be "Fine" To Keep Troops In Iraq For "A Hundred Years", 3/January/2008, http://www.motherjones.com/mojo/2008/0 1/mccain-nh-would-be-fine-keep-troops-iraq-hundred-years

16.  http://www.en.wikipedia.org/wiki/primi ng_(psychology)

17.  Sheldon Filger, Federal Reserve Begins Massive Monetization Of U.S. Government Debt, Huffington Post, 11/August/2010, http://www.huffingtonpost.com/sheldon_filg er/federal-reserve-begins-ma_b_677.483.html

18.  US Senate Roll Call Votes, http://www.senate.gov/legislative/lis/roll_cal

l_lists/roll_call_vote_cfm.cfm?congress=111
&session=2&vote=00016

19. http://www.en.wikipedia.org/wiki/nafta

20. http://www.cccarto.com/congress_map
s

21. http://www.en.wikipedia.org/wiki/abra
moff_scandal

22. http://www.en.wikipedia.org/wiki/assoc
iation_of_community_organizations_for_refo
rm_now

23. http://www.independentvoting.org/abo
ut/index.html